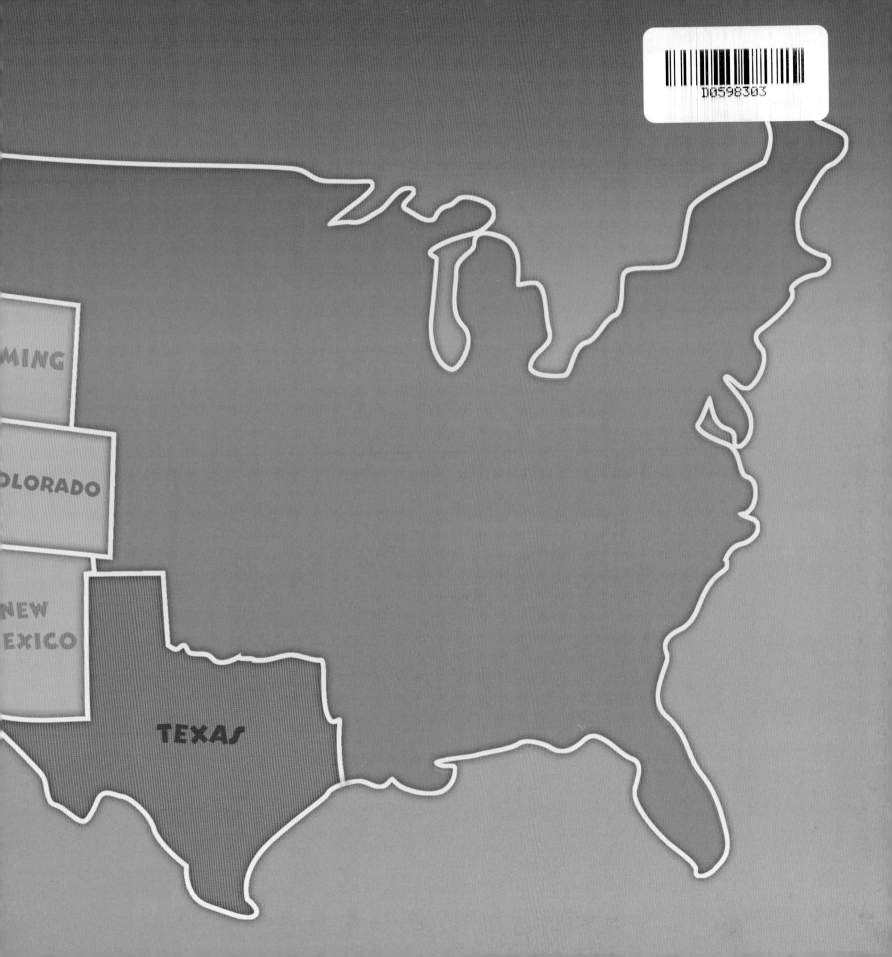

CIP data is available.

Published in the United States 2013 by

🍎 Blue Apple Books

515 Valley Street, Maplewood, NJ 07040

www.blueapplebooks.com

Printed in China

ISBN: 978-1-60905-354-3

1 3 5 7 9 10 8 6 4 2

TRAVELS with CHARLIE

Way Out West

MILES BACKER ★ *Illustrated by* **CHUCK NITZBERG**

BLUE 🍎 APPLE

You'll spy the Grand Canyon.

You'll find Jackson Hole.

You'll see Salt Lake City

and the Hollywood Bowl.

You'll spy Mt. McKinley

and Dinosaur Park

and a trail that was forged

by Lewis and Clark.

You'll see Carlsbad Caverns

and a ranch for old cars.

You'll spot Klamath Falls.

Can you guess where you are?

You'll spy a space needle,

a pineapple plantation,

and the great Hoover Dam

as you crisscross the nation,

following Charlie

wherever he goes.

He's off to the West.

Where is he?

Who knows!

Alaska THE LAST FRONTIER

Where are the Northern Lights

in the sky?

Where's Mt. McKinley,

where you'll see eagles fly?

Find Anchorage, Fairbanks,

Juneau, and Nome.

Find a town called North Pole

and an Eskimo home.

Where's Charlie?

NORTHERN LIGHTS

St. Lawrence Island

NORTH POLE

Mt. McKinley

Nome

Barrow
Eskimo Village

Nunivak Island

Yukon River

Fairbanks

Fort Yukon

Lake Iliamna

North American Championship Sled Dog Races

Aleutian Islands

Anchorage

Kodiak Island

Gold Rush Museum

Yukon Route Railroad

Juneau

Fjords

Totem Pole Heritage Center

Ketchikan

Arizona GRAND CANYON STATE

STATE CAPITAL
Phoenix

STATE FLAG

DID YOU KNOW...

- The original London Bridge was shipped stone by stone and reconstructed in Lake Havasu City.

- The Arizona ridge-nosed rattlesnake is perhaps the most beautiful of all eleven species of rattlesnakes found in Arizona.

- The world's largest solar telescope is located at Kitts Peak National Observatory in the city of Sells.

- Tombstone, Ruby, Gillette, and Gunsight are among the ghost towns scattered throughout the state.

- At one time camels were used to transport goods across Arizona.

- Arizona (along with Hawaii and part of Indiana) does not observe Daylight Savings Time.

Where's the Grand Canyon?

Where's an old copper mine?

Where's a meteor crater

and a petrified pine?

Find Flagstaff and Phoenix

and two reservations,

homes of the Apache

and Navajo nations.

Where's Charlie?

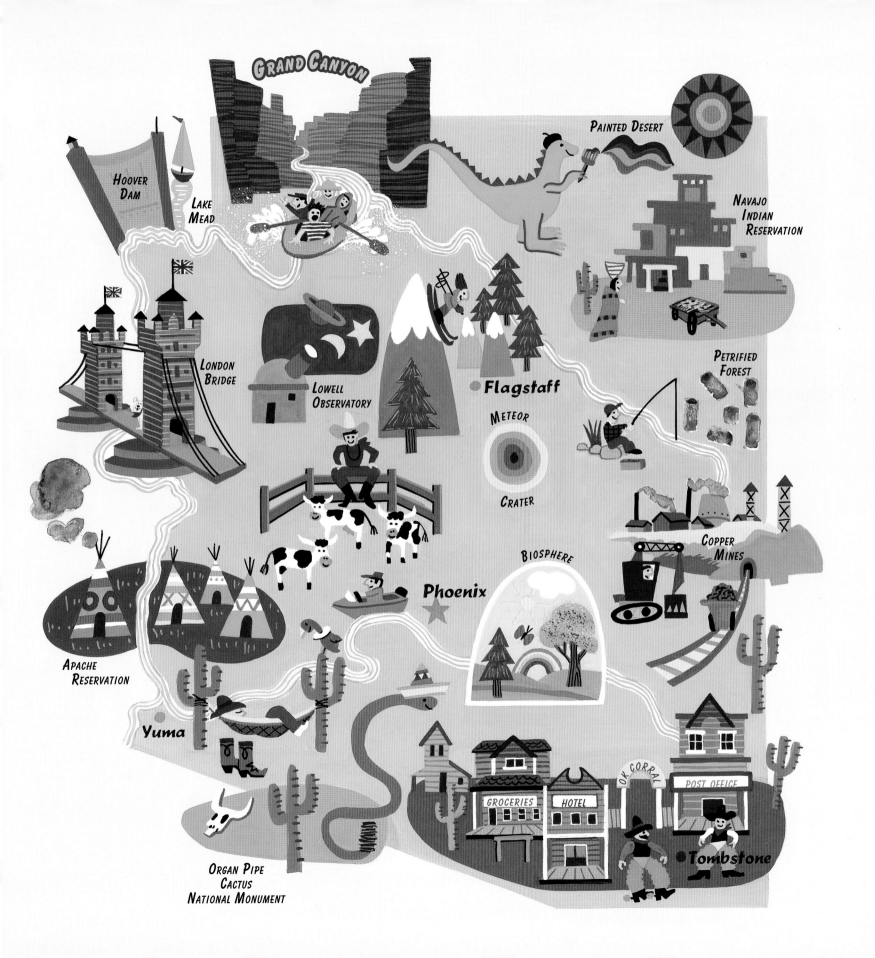

California *THE GOLDEN STATE*

STATE CAPITAL
Sacramento

STATE FLAG

DID YOU KNOW . . .

- Some of the giant redwoods in Sequoia National Park are more than 2,000 years old.

- More than 300,000 tons of grapes are grown annually in California.

- Death Valley is recognized as the hottest, driest place in the United States. It isn't uncommon for the summer temperatures to reach more than 115 degrees.

- The Hollywood Bowl is the world's largest outdoor amphitheater.

- The first permanent motion picture theater opened in Los Angeles on April 2, 1902.

Where's the Golden Gate Bridge?

Where's a beach? Where's a zoo?

I can find Tahoe

and Palm Springs. Can you?

Find San Francisco

and the Hollywood Bowl.

Find Napa. Find a surfer.

Find a tree with a hole.

Where's Charlie?

Colorado *THE CENTENNIAL STATE*

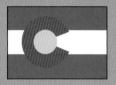

Where's Royal Gorge Bridge?

Where's Dinosaur Park?

Where's Black Canyon,

a famous landmark?

Find the Colorado River,

flowing with trout.

Find Great Sand Dunes

and a moose camping out.

Where's Charlie?

DINOSAUR NATIONAL PARK

COLORADO RIVER

Denver

PIKES PEAK

WORLD FIGURE
SKATING MUSEUM
AND HALL OF FAME

Colorado Springs

Aspen

SKI SCHOOL

Royal Gorge
Bridge

LAKE ISABEL

BLACK CANYON

ARKANSAS RIVER

PREHISTORIC
CLIFF
DWELLINGS

BALANCED
ROCK

GREAT SAND DUNES
NATIONAL MONUMENT

MESA VERDE NATIONAL PARK

ROCKY MOUNTAINS

Hawaii THE ALOHA STATE

STATE CAPITAL
Honolulu

STATE FLAG

DID YOU KNOW . . .

- The state of Hawaii consists of eight main islands: Niihau, Kauai, Oahu, Maui, Molokai, Lanai, Kahoolawe, and the big island of Hawaii.

- There are only 12 letters in the Hawaiian alphabet.
  Vowels: A, E, I, O, U
  Consonants: H, K, L, M, N, P, W

- The world's largest wind generator is on the island of Oahu. The windmill has two blades 400 feet long. They sit on the top of a tower twenty stories high.

- Haleakala Crater (Ha-lay-ah-ka-lah) is the world's largest dormant volcano.

- Hulopoe Bay is a marine preserve and is considered one of the best diving spots in the world.

- The island of Molokai contains the world's highest sea cliffs, Hawaii's longest waterfall, and the largest white sand beach in the state.

Where in the sea

can you stand next to sharks?

Where is Oahu?

Where's Volcano Park?

Find Lanai Plantation.

Find dolphins at play,

palm trees, Pearl Harbor,

and then find a lei.

Where's Charlie?

NIIHAU LIGHTHOUSE

HAUULA FALLS

NIIHAU

KAUAI

OAHU

Pearl Harbor

Honolulu

MOLOKAI

LANAI

Lanai Pineapple Plantation

KAHOOLAWE

MAUI

MAUNA LOA

VOLCANO NATIONAL PARK

HANAUMA BAY REEF

HAWAII

Rain Forest

Hilo

Idaho THE GEM STATE

Where's Lava Hot Springs

and historic Fort Hall?

Where is Sun Valley

where some skiers fall?

Find a trail that was forged

by Lewis and Clark.

Find Twin Falls and

Ponderosa State Park.

Where's Charlie?

BIRDS OF PREY NATIONAL CONSERVATION AREA

SCHWEITZER SKI BASIN

WORLD POTATO EXPO

THE LEWIS AND CLARK TRAIL

HYDROPLANE RACES

HELLS CANYON

PONDEROSA STATE PARK

SUN VALLEY RESORT

WORLD'S LARGEST POTATO

★ Boise

CRATERS OF THE MOON

Blackfoot

Pocatello

Fort Hall

SAWTOOTH NATIONAL FOREST

BALANCE ROCK

LAVA HOT SPRINGS

TWIN FALLS

Nevada THE SILVER STATE

STATE CAPITAL
Carson City

STATE FLAG

DID YOU KNOW...

- Once the highest concrete dam in the world, Hoover Dam is 726 feet high and 660 feet thick at its base. 13,000 to 16,000 people cross the dam every day.

- Berlin-Ichthyosaur State Park is constructed around the fossilized remains of ancient, mysterious reptiles within a well-preserved, turn-of-the-century Nevada mining camp.

- Las Vegas has more hotel rooms than any other place on earth.

- Nevada is the largest gold-producing state in the nation.

- In Death Valley, the Kangaroo Rat can live its entire life without drinking a drop of liquid.

Where is Death Valley?

Where are palm trees?

Where's Pyramid Lake,

where a girl water-skis?

Find Carson City,

and Hoover Dam,

Las Vegas, Reno,

and a bighorn ram.

Where's Charlie?

New Mexico LAND OF ENCHANTMENT

STATE CAPITAL
Santa Fe

STATE FLAG

DID YOU KNOW...

- Each October Albuquerque hosts the world's largest international hot air balloon fiesta.

- The Rio Grande is New Mexico's longest river and runs the entire length of New Mexico.

- Tens of thousands of bats live in the Carlsbad Caverns. The largest chamber of Carlsbad Caverns is more than 10 football fields long and about 22 stories high.

- Elephant Butte Reservoir, created by a dam constructed in 1916 across the Rio Grande, is 40 miles long with more than 200 miles of shoreline.

- The Jemez Mountains are a volcanic field in north central New Mexico that overlies the west edge of the Rio Grande rift. These volcanoes are considered dormant but will probably erupt sometime in the future.

Where's the Santa Fe Trail?

Where's a rodeo ride?

Find Carlsbad Caverns,

where bats often hide.

Find a volcano,

dishes listening to space,

Los Alamos, and

a bird running a race.

Where's Charlie?

Oregon THE BEAVER STATE

Where are sea lion caves?

Where is Mt. Hood?

Where is a stage
where great actors have stood?

Find the Oregon Trail.

Find Klamath Falls.

Find the Pacific,
where a fishing boat trawls.

Where's Charlie?

Texas THE LONE STAR STATE

STATE CAPITAL
Austin

STATE FLAG

DID YOU KNOW...

- More wool comes from the state of Texas than any other state in the United States.

- The state's cattle population is estimated to be near 16 million.

- Port Lavaca has the world's longest fishing pier. Originally part of the causeway connecting the two sides of Lavaca Bay, the center span was destroyed by Hurricane Carla in 1961.

- The Tyler Municipal Rose Garden is the world's largest rose garden. It contains 38,000 rosebushes representing 500 varieties of roses set in a 22-acre garden.

- More species of bats live in Texas than in any other part of the United States.

- Hot sauce is such an important condiment in Texas that there are annual hot sauce festivals and contests in most major cities.

Where is El Paso?

Where is Big Bend?

Where can you go

on a ride with a friend?

Find Amarillo.

Find a ranch for old cars.

Find the place where we send

NASA rockets to Mars.

Where's Charlie?

CADILLAC RANCH

• Amarillo

CHILI

OIL FIELDS

El Paso

BUDDY HOLLY CENTER

Paris •

Dallas •

SIX FLAGS

NASA/
KENNEDY
SPACE CENTER

LONG HORN RANCH

WATERMELON FESTIVAL

LULING

BIG BEND

RIO GRANDE

THE ALAMO

Austin

Houston

TEXAS
BBQ

X-treme
HOT
HOT
HOT

HOT

DON'T
MESS
WITH

TEXAS

GULF
COAST

Utah

THE BEEHIVE STATE

Where is Lake Powell?

Where is Mystic Hot Springs?

Where is the temple

where the Mormon Choir sings?

Find Salt Lake City,

the Bonneville Flats,

Sundance Film Festival,

and dinosaurs with hats.

Where's Charlie?

Washington THE EVERGREEN STATE

STATE CAPITAL
Olympia

STATE FLAG

Did You Know...

- The northwesternmost point in the continental U.S. is Cape Flattery on Washington's Olympic Peninsula.

- The Governor Albert D. Rosellini Bridge at Evergreen Point is the longest floating bridge in the world. The bridge connects Seattle and Medina across Lake Washington.

- The oldest operating gas station in the United States is in Zillah.

- The highest point in Washington is Mount Rainier. It was named after Peter Rainier, a British soldier who fought against the Americans in the Revolutionary War.

- The state of Washington is the only state to be named after a United States president.

Where's the Space Needle?

Where's a great big whale?

Where's Puget Sound

and a place you can sail?

Find a volcano

without a top,

a museum for kites,

and a place apples drop.

Where's Charlie?

COLVILLE NATIONAL FOREST

HOH RAIN FOREST

SPACE NEEDLE

NORTH CASCADES

Monorail

OLYMPIC NATIONAL PARK

PUGET SOUND FERRY

GRAND COULEE DAM

Seattle

Spokane

MOSES LAKE SKATEBOARD PARK

Olympia

WORLD KITE MUSEUM

APPLE ORCHARDS

MT. RAINIER

MOSES LAKE

INTERNATIONAL KITE FESTIVAL

MT. SAINT HELENS

BIGFOOT

FORT WALLA WALLA

Wyoming THE EQUALITY STATE

STATE CAPITAL
Cheyenne

STATE FLAG

DID YOU KNOW...

- In 1872, Yellowstone National Park was named as the first national park in the world.

- Old Faithful, a geyser in Yellowstone National Park, is America's most famous. It shoots water into the air every 76 minutes.

- Devil's Tower was designated the first national monument by President Theodore Roosevelt in 1906.

- In 1869, Wyoming became the first state to grant women the right to vote.

- The largest coal mine in the U.S. is Black Thunder, located near Wright, Wyoming.

- In 1852, the first schoolhouse in Wyoming was built at Fort Laramie.

- Wyoming is home to the world's largest single elk herd.

- Cody, Wyoming, is named after William "Buffalo Bill" Cody.

Where's the Platte River?

Where's Jackson Hole?

Find a man on a mountain

with a long fishing pole.

Find Flaming Gorge.

Find Devil's Tower.

Now find Old Faithful,

a geyser with power.

Where's Charlie?

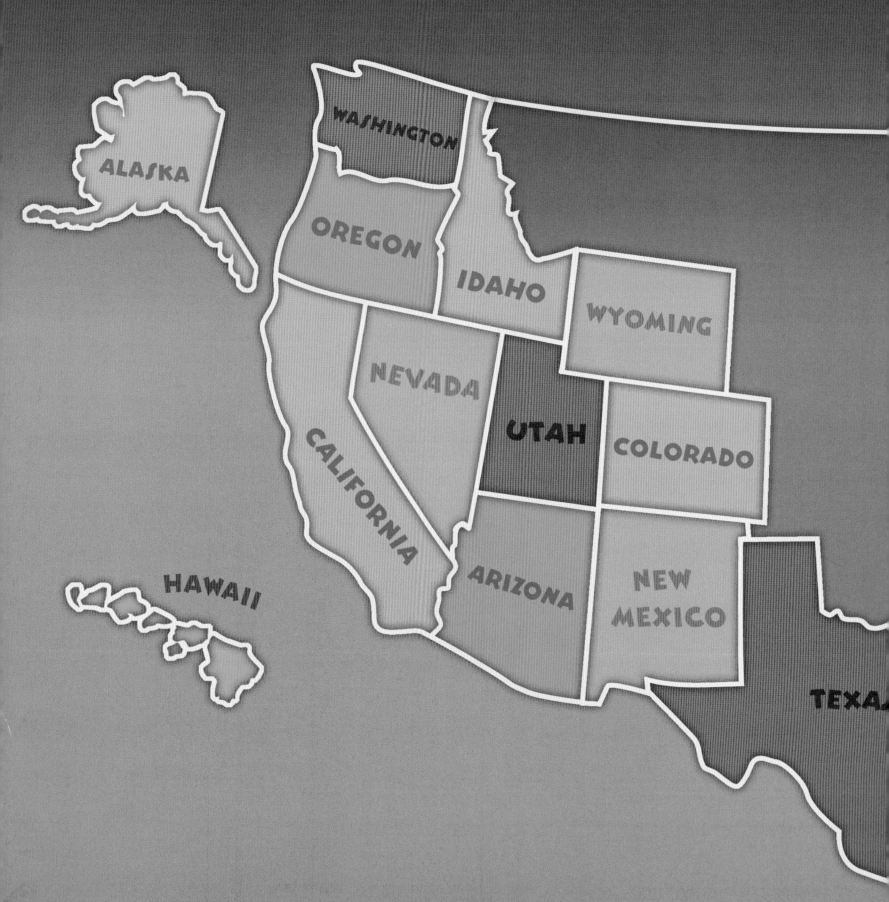